RADICAL CLARITY FOR BUSINESS

How to Empower People for Better Results at Work

Clifford Jones

Printed in the United States of America

First Printing, 2020

ISBN: 978-1-7360191-1-5

Clifford Jones
Clarity Strategic Advisors, LLC
20343 N. Hayden Road, Suite 105
Scottsdale, AZ 85255, Scottsdale, AZ 85255

www.CliffordJones.com

Dedication

To God, my mother, father, and family. Thank you. I love you.

Table of Contents

PART ONE – INTRODUCTION & OVERVIEW

CHAPTER 1: THE POWER OF CLARITY

"Champions aren't made in gyms. Champions are made from something they have deep inside them—a desire, a dream, a vision. They have to have the skill and the will. But the will must be stronger than the skill."

— Muhammad Ali

If you're a business owner or leader who gets stuck once in a while and is looking for a more effective way to get better business results, this book is for you. The best way to get unstuck is to find clarity. When you're clear about what you want, and how to get there, you've got confidence.

The key for your business is making sure everyone shares the same clarity and confidence you do. When that happens, people feel better about doing their jobs. You're more likely to achieve your goals with less cost, work, and stress.

It doesn't matter what size company you run, or how many people you employ directly, and as subcontractors, everyone who seeks to lead a healthier, more-balanced, and less-stressful work life can benefit from reading *Radical Clarity for Business*.

The only requirement for getting at least one massive benefit from this book is that you truly desire to empower your people for better results. If you think you can build a successful business on your own, this book can't help you as much.

You also need a willing and open mindset for learning new ways to improve yourself and empower your people. Naturally, you want the same to be true for anyone on your team you invite to help you create and execute your strategic plan of action.

Strategic Planning Is Essential

Did you know that only 53 of the Fortune 500 remain on the list from 1955?[1] That's how tough it is to sustain business success. They can't afford not to take strategic action planning seriously. That's why large, long-term profitable companies use strategic plans, processes, systems, and technology mapped to success measures.

Imagine what this means for small and midsize business owners and the people who work for us. We would be complete fools to not take strategic planning and score keeping seriously considering the odds against us. Alignment of people through planning, communication, commitment, and accountability is how to get better results.

Whether you already have a strategic plan in place or not, Clarity can help you get better results by laser-focusing on ways to

---

[1] https://www.aei.org/carpe-diem/only-52-us-companies-have-been-on-the-fortune-500-since-1955-thanks-to-the-creative-destruction-that-fuels-economic-prosperity/

strengthen your brand, be more mindful for marketing results, and empower your sales and customer service people to reach their full potential. In fact, the biggest and most-costly mistakes we see when facilitating and coaching business owners, leaders, and teams happen in the branding and go-to-market action planning sections of this book.

You'll get to all of that soon enough. For now, sit down and commit to learning how to get more clarity and confidence yourself, and by sharing it with everyone at work. When everyone works with confidence, you're more likely to get better results.

Clarity Is A Process You Can Trust

Clarity for Business is about helping you lead and manage your business without losing your mind or your shirt. Being in business can be stressful. There are over 30 million small businesses in America, and they are the heart and soul of our nation.

One of the biggest differences about the Clarity strategic action planning process is our ability to help you understand the massive power of your inner game. Your inner game as a business owner, leader, and manager has two parts; your conscious and subconscious mind.

When you and your people learn to tap into the power of both, you'll get results like you've never seen before. You'll get a thorough understanding of ways to improve your inner game throughout this book. At the end of the book, you'll see a list of healthy habits you can practice for maintaining clarity and confidence.

Not having clarity about your potential options for business success can be stressful. If you're stuck in your business and not sure how to get better results, focus on finishing the book and a first draft of your new strategic plan.

In most cases, business owners can read the book and write the first draft of the new strategic plan within a few hours. The more you practice working "on" your business strategically, the easier it will be to work "in" your business tactically. Read every chapter, complete the action step at the end, and you're on your way to getting clarity, confidence and better results.

Now would be a great time to find a new notebook, or create a digital document you can use to take notes. Each chapter will guide you through writing your own strategic plan of action. Once you get the hang of the process, you can get the planning work done with your people in one hour each week.

Go as far as you can on your own the first time through. Later, invite the people on your team who can help you the most. Invite each person when you feel confident telling them about the process. It is also a great idea to make sure they get a copy of my book and read it with you.

The sooner you invite your people to share the planning process with you, the faster you will get their buy in.

How to Get Unstuck

Nobody likes to feel stuck in their job or uncertain about what the future holds. Most people agree, building a successful business is about hiring the right people, and trusting them to do a good job. Help your people overcome the dysfunctions of a team by including them in your business planning process.

We suggest using Clarity strategic action planning for internal purposes only. If you need a more formal business plan for external use such as raising money from investors, or getting a bank loan, doing so will be easy once you have your Clarity strategic action plan completed.

Clarity keeps you and your people from getting stuck. Everyone will always know the expected results and willingly commit to their part of the plan. Creating a culture of accountability is the best way to foster trust.

If you get stuck in the strategic planning process, ask us for help. You can easily schedule a complimentary strategy session with one of our certified coaches by going to my website at www.CliffordJones.com.

You will soon be able to state your mission, vision, purpose, goals, drivers, and the critical accountabilities for everyone on your team. They will all feel as if they are part of your plan, boosting clarity and confidence. When you don't have clarity and confidence in your strategy, and your team has not bought into the shared plan of action, results will suffer.

This book will help you reduce costs and stress. You should be able to get more done in less time. Each chapter will take you closer to better results. You're on your way to being more efficient and empowering your people with process.

Why I Wrote This Book

Failing in business is painful. When I was 12 years old, I watched my father's hotel and restaurant business collapse. Along with the business's failure, my father no longer had an income to support our family, including me, my younger sister, brother, and mother.

I'll never forget feeling the terror within as I watched my parents reinvent themselves into their next new business venture. The fall out of grace was rather sudden, and the necessity to develop new business was urgent. My father and mother started a residential real estate business and got back on their feet after a few years.

As a kid, I vowed to be successful in business. My parents were heroes to me and set the perfect example of how to pursue your dreams, overcome obstacles, raise a happy family, and be successful.

I kept my vow to be a successful business owner, and it wasn't always easy. I failed many times over the last 30 years. Everything you're about to learn comes from direct experience starting, funding, growing, and selling two small businesses.

Make It Easier to Follow You

Do you need a strategic plan to be successful? Unless your name is Steve Jobs, yes.

Most business owners agree that our business is our best and most important investment. For me and millions of others, we put everything we owned on the line. We had to find ways to succeed, fail forward, and bounce back.

Having a great strategic plan makes it easier for everyone to follow you. Your plan serves as the blueprint or roadmap during good times, and it prepares you for anything that might lie ahead.

Why is it so many business owners don't have a written strategic plan even though they agree having one is important for empowering people and competing effectively? Why do business owners who put everything on the line believe we can wing it without a legitimate process for success? Most of the time the excuse, "I'm too busy." In other words, planning for success simply isn't a priority, nor is being disciplined.

If nobody knows exactly where you're going, and they don't have a roadmap, how can you expect people to follow you and feel great about doing their jobs? You can't.

Being in business has its highs and lows. Without a strong foundation in brand, marketing, sales, and finance, we're prone to fail hard when the unexpected strikes. As a younger business owner, I had no clue how to get myself out of the mess. I had sold my first business to a Wall Street brokerage firm, and shortly following, I was broke and broken.

At my lowest, I was ready to give up. Then, after struggling to find a way to start a new business, I had a "moment of clarity." I stopped beating myself up for my failures. I got help from professionals, family, and closest friends. Because of what you're going to learn in this book, my life changed forever. Clarity helped me get back on track, build, and sell another business. Now I get to coach and empower other coaches, owners, and leaders.

Why should you believe anything I write? Because Clarity worked for me out of necessity. When I was younger, I let stress almost wipe me out more than once. In starting, funding, leading, managing, growing, and selling two small businesses, I lost my money, faith, health, and sense of direction. But with clarity, I could bounce back.

What to Expect

There are three parts to *Clarity for Business,* including 17 chapters. Read the chapters, take notes, and complete the suggested action steps at the end of each chapter.

The first three chapters set the stage for active, strategic planning, and how your inner game makes a difference. You'll also learn the difference between clarity and radical clarity; the pinnacle of peak performance.

The more you work with Clarity strategic action planning, the easier it will be to overcome obstacles, including the unexpected. When you achieve radical clarity, or peak performance, your business and life may seem effortless.

In chapter four, you'll learn a simple way to assess the clarity and alignment of your current people. Read a list of 10 brief statements about your organization. You'll assign a score of 1-10, 10 meaning you strongly agree with the statement.

At the end, you'll total the numbers for your overall "Clarity Score." Your Clarity Score shows alignment. Alignment is important because it helps your people feel empowered and confident. You will learn to plan and align everyone better.

The higher your Clarity Score, the easier it is to get results. Most times, you will see cost reductions, workflow simplification, streamlining, and efficiencies within 90 days or fewer. Think like a champion and expect to win.

Part two of *Clarity for Business* is where you draft your strategic plan. In chapter five, you'll learn how to better set goals with intention. Chapters 6-11 set the stage for you to do serious branding and go-to-market planning. It's during these chapters that you could experience some breakthroughs.

In chapter 12, you'll get a refresher on how to hire with your head using performance-based hiring. Then, in chapters 13 and 14, you'll complete your plan by assigning measures of success. By the time you're done sharing your strategic planning process with your people, they'll feel empowered, and you'll be on your way to a culture of accountability, commitment, and results.

Part three will help you pull all the pieces of your new strategic action plan together and live it every day. In chapters 15-17, you'll read about healthy habits for improving your inner game. Implement your new habits and experience the benefits of Clarity strategic action planning.

Your Blueprint for Success

Can you imagine building the Golden Gate bridge without a blueprint or plan of action to keep everyone aligned? No. And you probably wouldn't want to drive across a bridge built by someone who flew by the seat of their pants.

The same is true with building a successful business. Most leaders agree that when we cannot plan, we plan to fail. Reaching goals is about aligning a sound strategy with the right people, then working together, and feeling empowered to win.

The best way to plan for clarity is to focus on what is most essential. You determine appropriate goals, three pillars or core drivers, action steps, and objectives. The best way to get alignment is to invite your executive team after you've read the book. Plug them in so they can read the book and see the plan structure. Let them ask questions and help you improve it. You never know where great ideas might happen when you embrace diversity and inclusion.

Eventually, we suggest inviting everyone in your company to know about the plan, and ideally take part in it at some level. The goal is to find ways for aligning people with their department, roles, and responsibilities. Building a company is a team and contact sport, so make sure your lines of communication are wide open at all times.

Plan to hold weekly, one-hour operational meetings. You can review results often, including your monthly financial statements. You may host formal strategic planning meetings once a quarter, but that is up to you. Align your Clarity strategic action planning with training, coaching, and developing your people, and you'll get better results.

Empower Everyone to Be Better Leaders

We believe anyone can be a better leader or team player, given the awareness, mindset, and desire. Clarity is an ongoing process that empowers leaders on your team to know where you're going as a team or organization. You will learn to work better "on" your business and "on" the leadership mindset that fosters alignment, commitment, and results.

Clarity is unique in the way we approach teaching you the inner game for developing everyone's leadership mindset. Let's define leadership based on the book, *Neuroscience for Leadership: Harnessing the Brain Gain Advantage* by Tara Swart, Kitty Chisholm, and Paul Brown.

"Leaders are individuals who have sufficient status, power, dominance, and influence in a group to achieve innovatory goals with and through others."

The difference between leaders who get results and those who languish in mediocrity comes down to mindset, values, commitments, and habits. When everyone on your team shares a can-do attitude and they have the tools they need, you'll get more done in less time.

Believe in yourself and your people. If not, change as needed. Commit. Dr. Bruce Lipton, Ph.D., is the author of *The Biology of Belief* and a pioneer in epigenetics, the science of the mindset and beliefs we carry. Once you work on the process that follows, your faith in your ability to get results will shift into a higher gear.

Clarity Strategic Planning Overview

Here's a high-level overview of what lies ahead for you. Remember, the power of process is a cornerstone for empowering people to align and get better results. The way to get the best results is to make Clarity strategic planning a habit.

Here are some systems and resources you can use to organize your new strategic plan.

1. A single, shared strategic plan document. If you care about your business, care about how you document your blueprint for success. We prefer Google Suite and Drive.
2. A calendar such as Google Calendar, Microsoft 365, and iCal from Apple. You'll start scheduling new meetings as needed.
3. Spreadsheets, task managers, and list managers are available on your smartphone and computer to organize your plan to meet your needs.
4. Project management and communication systems such as Basecamp, Trello, and Slack.
5. Email systems like Constant Contact or MailChimp.
6. A simple CRM solution like Pipedrive.
7. Web meeting solutions such as Google Meet, Skype, Zoom.

There's no such thing as the perfect business plan. Don't worry about getting your plan right the first time through. Over time, the process will become as natural as breathing.

Imagine your mission, vision, and goals are clear. Everybody buys in. They have the skill and tools to do their jobs. You see better results in communication, team morale, productivity, workplace satisfaction, and engagement when everyone shares the same clarity and confidence.

Think about creating a culture of accountability. Everyone commits and trusts each other. Why would you want to stop enjoying the benefits of strategic action planning once you see the difference it makes? Practice clarity often.

Action Step: *Get a notebook or pad of paper, turn off your phone, and get ready to learn the fundamentals so you can apply one key lesson you learn from each part of this book.*

CHAPTER 2: LEADING PEOPLE WITH CLARITY

"permanence, perseverance, and persistence in spite of all obstacles, discouragement, and impossibilities: It is this, that in all things distinguishes the strong soul from the weak."

—Thomas Carlyle

Leadership Matters

Business and career success are a game of confidence. It's important to know that the process you're about to begin never fails. Only the people who cannot practice the process cannot get results.

Most leaders who own companies agree that human capital is our most significant investment in a business. Let's also agree that everyone you employ is a direct reflection of your leadership ability. This chapter will help you become more aware of how you're showing up as a leader, and what it takes to inspire and motivate others better.

When you lead with clarity, you get results because you know what not to do. You can be more efficient by being more focused. Imagine what will happen to results when everyone feels empowered to do their job with the least supervision possible. Share the Clarity strategic planning process with your people and watch them lead themselves.

Getting Started with Clarity

Before we dive into ways to improve your inner game, leadership skills, and business results, here are some things you need to get started.

1. **Time.** You need to commit time to work "on" your business by completing the book and your first plan draft. After that, you will invite others to learn about the process. Once you have a solid plan in place, invest one hour a week in working on the execution of your action steps. Following that, you may host more formal, quarterly meetings with your executive team.
2. **Documentation.** You'll need a digital document or notebook you can use to take notes, write, and edit your first strategic plan of action. Ideally, the document is simple to share and edit with others who you invite to plan. This document becomes your strategic action plan.
3. **Belief.** Believe in yourself, your business or career, and the people you work with essential well-being investments. When self-doubt comes, you'll be better prepared to help yourself. Clarity works.

4. **Goals; desire.** What do you want specifically? Focus on it. See, feel, and trust your passion and purpose for achieving your mission and vision.

5. **Purpose.** The more significant and more definite your purpose, the more likely it is you will succeed. The same is true for your people. Hire people empowered by an ambition to align with your company purpose.

6. **Commitment.** Commitment is keeping your word long after the feeling you had when you committed wears off. Maintain a commitment to learn, grow, be coachable, and become a better leader every day. Commitment, accountability, and trust are essential.

7. **People.** When you are ready, invite the right people to be part of the planning process. Be inclusive. Start with your executive and core teams. Expand from there as it makes sense for your business.

Workers Aren't Engaged (Happy)

How engaged and happy is everyone in your organization, and how do you know? If you haven't conducted strategic planning, performance reviews, behavioral, personality, stress, and 360 degree feedback surveys, maybe there's room for improvement. If so, you'll start by measuring what's happening now, then develop action steps to train, coach, and empower your people.

It's easy to understand recent surveys about workplace performance and engagement reveal that most workers aren't engaged at work. The primary reasons include poor hiring practices, ineffective training and supervision, no coaching programs, inappropriate compensation, misfit of values and culture, and more.

You'll learn in a later chapter the importance of performance-based hiring for empowering people. For now, realize that workplace dysfunction begins with a lack of focus and alignment to the common goal. Poor communication, limited accountability to a shared plan, and lack of trust are byproducts. By being aware of the things that hold teams back, you can create action steps to overcome almost anything.

Peak Worker Productivity

Did you know that peak worker productivity in America is only 17%, and the peak happened decades ago? It turns out, maybe we aren't as productive as we think.[2]

Despite the many advances in technology and workplace innovation, something big has to change if you want big changes in productivity. Leadership and empowering people to be aware of the power of their inner game are the two keys for most of us. We have to empower people to be engaged, which means they enjoy their work. And we have to help people be as productive as possible, while minimizing the negative impact of ongoing stress.

There is typically tons of room for improvement in mindset. Personally, I see the subconscious mind as the last frontier we need to explore to create more productive, engaged, aligned workers. Despite the ongoing negative rants of mainstream media, there is lots of good news to report such as major advances in technology, biology, and human performance. In fact, we will experience the next

---

[2] https://www.youtube.com/watch?v=QX3M8Ka9vUA

industrial revolution in the decades ahead; the Internet of Things, IoT.

Jeremy Rifkin is the author of the book, *The Third Industrial Revolution*. On his website he writes, "The price of energy and food is climbing, unemployment remains high, the housing market has tanked, consumer and government debt is soaring, and the recovery is slowing. Facing the prospect of a second collapse of the global economy, humanity is desperate for a sustainable economic game plan to take us into the future."

Rifkin shares his five pillars for creating thousands of new businesses and millions of new jobs as we shift our thinking from hierarchical power to flat, lateral power. Empowering our people with clarity and confidence can give you a massive competitive advantage.[3]

Here are Rifkin's five pillars.[4]
1. Shifting to Renewable Energy
2. Converting Buildings into Power Plants
3. Hydrogen and Other Energy Storage Technology
4. Smart Grid Technology
5. Plug in, Electric, Hybrid, and Fuel Cell based Transportation

Strategic action planning, ongoing meetings, your ongoing project management, and internal communications determine the extent to which your people can and will get their jobs done right the first time. Leaders bear the burden of the team from the first point of contact—recruiting. After that, your onboarding process,

---

[3] https://www.foet.org/books/the-third-industrial-revolution/
[4] https://wiki.p2pfoundation.net/Third_Industrial_Revolution

leadership development, and coaching of talent and teams must kick into top gear.

Cultivate Leadership Awareness with Coaching

We believe everyone has the potential to improve their leadership ability, even if they are leading themselves. Most of us work in groups. The more effective we are working in small teams, the easier it is to produce better results.

It's up to us as owners, leaders, and managers to find effective ways to empower the people we employ. Investing in coaching and learning opportunities is one way to show your people you believe in them.

As an example, the president of one company we coach told his top leaders that he was "giving them a gift" by paying for a coaching program to help them become better leaders.

The benefit of investing in our people is we show them that it's possible to learn and improve together. Failing is safe in the context of a team that is aligned and empowered. Most business owners like me lead, manage, fix the computer, and take out the trash if we must. We are willing to do anything to help our people feel empowered. I see everyone as a leader, and treat them as such. My wife and I treated our sons as adults before they became adults. That helped become better adults sooner.

Here's an excellent definition for a leader from John P. Kotter[5], a professor at Harvard Business School [6]:

---

[5] https://www.hbs.edu/faculty/Pages/profile.aspx?facId=6495
[6] https://www.sagepub.com/sites/default/files/upm-binaries/33554_Chapter1.pdf

"Leadership is, most fundamentally, about changes. What leaders do is create the systems and organizations that managers need, and, eventually, elevate them up to a whole new level or ... change in some basic ways to take advantage of new opportunities."

Coach your people to be better coaches at all levels. When you think about it, replacing negative self-talk with positive self-talk is a form of self-coaching or conditioning of our minds. Learning to coach can make a dramatic difference when you learn how to meld it with leadership and management.

Can you imagine a championship team leaving anyone out of the coaching and training process? Everyone who works for you deserves to be part of your Clarity strategic planning process at some point. You'll know how to get there. Keep trusting the process and finish the book.

The Power of Discovery

Clarity as a process includes asking intelligent questions and learning as a team. Here are some discovery questions to help you improve your self-awareness as a leader.

1. **What kind of leader are you?** Commitment and accountability foster trust and improve performance. One way to measure your leadership ability is to ask the people following you. You can ask people informally and see what you get. It's often a best practice to use professional assessments, including 360 Feedback Surveys.

2. **What results are you achieving?** If you're not hitting the goal, it's essential to be objective and get to the root cause with solutions.

3. **What's working well?** Compliment and encourage yourself and your team on what's working well. Reinforce what's working.

4. **What's not working, missing?** Discuss what's not working well, and what's missing.

5. **What needs to change next?** Change is uncomfortable for most humans. Get used to it through conditioning your mind.

6. **What are the most important actions to take for best results?** Awareness, talent, and experience are keys. Choose your action steps by prioritizing more carefully.

When you commit to being a better leader, you'll do the work to make improvements. You'll invest in coaching, training, and other ways to empower yourself and your people.

Ask intelligent questions with an open heart and mind. Learn to listen more actively by caring about others around you, and investing in them with time and attention. Empower everyone to win.

Action Step: *Evaluate your current team. Update your organization chart. Consider how you could improve the work environment. Reflect on simple habits you can develop, such as active listening, being calmer, and more patient. Ask yourself what's working, not working, missing, and next for action steps?*

CHAPTER 3: THE INNER GAME OF CLARITY

"One of the things I learned the hard way was that it doesn't pay to get discouraged. Keeping busy and making optimism a way of life can restore your faith in yourself."

—Lucille Ball

Throughout the rest of the book, I'm going to give you the most powerful discovery questions I've used to help hundreds of companies get better results over the last 15 years. I learned the most about digital marketing, content, marketing automation, and CRM solutions while building and managing my digital marketing agency, Conversion Marketing Experts, LLC.

I sold the agency to focus on training, coaching, and empowering other business owners, coaches, and leaders. I love the focus on growing Clarity Strategic Advisors, LLC because we're expanding the fastest by licensing, coaching, and empowering other successful business coaches and trusted, strategic advisors, and consultants.

Create A Culture for Learning

One key to your success is creating a culture for learning what's working, what's not working, what's missing, and what next. The only way to know what you don't know is by being open to new ideas and willing to learn and adapt constantly.

The point of this chapter is to reinforce why and how culture, coaching, training, and awareness of business fundamentals along with inner game transformation habits, you can most definitely drive better business results when you focus on empowering the right people to work with you.

How to Be More Competent

You're striving for competence. Learning drives competence. There are several stages of learning we need to reinforce in our organizations. Reinforce learning and watch people grow.

Martin M. Broadwell is a management consultant created "the four levels of teaching" in February 1969. The four levels suggest that we are unaware, unconscious, of our incompetence.[7] That explains why most workers self-rate their job performance higher than their supervisors and peers. The good news is we can learn to be competent through training, coaching, and planning.

Do you remember learning how to drive a car? At first, you knew you were a new driver because the car you trained in screamed, "Student Driver" all over it. No wonder other drivers steered clear of

---

[7] https://en.wikipedia.org/wiki/Four_stages_of_competence

you. You had to concentrate with everything you had to keep the car on the road safely.

The more you drove your car, the easier it became. Now, think about a time you were driving and your mind drifted off to something other than the road ahead of you. Where did you go? And who was driving the car? Your subconscious mind. You were temporarily unconsciously competent because your car can't drive itself unless you own a Tesla.

Learning is the key to competence. You eventually learn to do things on autopilot. That's when your subconscious runs the show, just like when you sleep and forget to breathe.

Here are the four stages of competence. Create a culture of constant learning and train your people to be more competent.

1. **Unconscious incompetence.** You don't know how to do something and you don't know it. You don't know what you don't know. In order to know you don't know something, you think about doing it. You must learn.
2. **Conscious incompetence.** You don't know how to do something, and you know it. You didn't learn from failing, for example. You see value in learning to be competent. You seek help with coaching and training, knowing you need it.
3. **Conscious competence.** You know how to do something. However, you must concentrate like when you're first learning to drive a car. You know what to do to get better. You may need a coach, trainer, or teacher.
4. **Unconscious competence.** At this stage of competence, you can eat a sandwich and talk on the cell phone while driving your car. You've had so much practice doing something it has

become "second nature." You're so good at the activity, and may be able to teach it to others. You could be a master at this level.

None of us know what we don't know. We gain clarity and confidence with experience. Humble up, leaders! You're learning like a champion and setting the example for your people.

Failure and Pain Make Great Teachers

Clarity is about empowering yourself and your people. Naturally, it makes sense to begin with you if you own or lead a company. Failure and pain are both great teachers when we are willing to learn the lesson and do the work to adapt.

If you've ever failed to reach a goal you desired deeply, you know the pain of confronting problems, obstacles, and unexpected roadblocks. The same is valid for pain. Listen to it and adapt your mental toughness; be more resilient by practicing and learning from mistakes.

Failure can cause stress when the mind is untrained to deal with it. Enduring stress without a mindful approach to managing your inner game can cause serious health issues. Stress, anxiety, depression, and all their health consequences are crushing us. America successfully reversed the life expectancy of its citizens for the third year in a row!

How does that happen in the wealthiest nation in the world? Many would suggest we've got our priorities screwed up. You can't control the world. You can control your mind, choices, and habits. Condition your mindset and empower yourself by striving for clarity and never stop practicing.

Mindset comes from core values and beliefs, conscious and not. All humans have biases and blind spots. By tapping into the behavioral science that drives us. Your mindset must be focused, committed, and passionate about empowering people to work with you.

Causes of Stress

Here is a list of common causes of stress. Observe how stress is showing up for you and your people. Then, you can choose additional action steps for better results.

1. **Demand Stress:** Poorly designed jobs and poor job fit cause demand stress.
2. **Efforts/Rewards Stress:** High output in your job drives minimal reward or result, causing stress.
3. **Control Stress:** High responsibilities at work, combined with low authority, causes control stress.
4. **Organization Change Stress:** Changes and poorly communicated or inconsistent policies increase stress.
5. **Manager/Supervisor Stress:** Your superior enormously pressures you, causing stress.
6. **Social Support Stress:** Lack of support and over-competitiveness from your team causes social support stress.
7. **Job Security Stress:** You fear losing your job. You never feel safe at work.

Make Stress Your Friend

How much does stress affect you and your people? How do you measure it so you can take proper measures before something goes wrong like higher absenteeism, workplace injuries, and other things that hold you back? Make your enemy your friend.

Stress can be your friend once you know how to use tools for improving your inner game. Did you know that stress-related ailments cost the nation $300 billion every year in medical bills and lost productivity?

How much is stress costing you, and what are you doing about it to stay healthy? One of the biggest benefits of the Clarity process is helping everyone on the team reduce stress. Our process helps you focus on what to do by helping you know what not to do.

When we look at the example set by the most successful athletes, leaders, entertainers, and artists, it's all about authenticity. Being authentic as a leader means your head, heart, and soul are working in alignment. The power of an authentic leader's purpose motivates them to train, stress their bodies and minds, recover, and compete at the highest level of their fields.

Measuring Stress

The first step to dealing with stress is measuring it. Too much stress leads to anxiety and many other health issues. Stress blocks clear thinking. Therefore, stress blocks clarity.

One of Clarity's most popular assessment tools is the Stress Quotient™ Assessment by Target Training International. It's a highly cost-effective scientific assessment for gauging causes of team and worker stress. They license my firm to administer the assessment, and we use it as a powerful coaching tool.

When you know what causes people stress and develop the toolkit and team to help you win the game, you're much more likely to be a more reliable leader. Over time, stress becomes your friend. It teaches you how to train, practice, and recover. The only way to get clarity is to work toward it as a more mindful, aware, caring leader who stays the course.

The Power of Process

You can't solve a problem at the place you created it. You must learn to step away from your problems, observe the situation, and make better conscious choices about your activities. Clarity strategic action planning is the best way to work on your business, and you need to be resilient.

We base every aspect of our strategic planning on practical application years, helping hundreds of teams get better results. Clarity incorporates spaced repetition learning, online technologies, and the neuroscience of leadership transformation. That's why our remote coaching programs for owners and teams are built in 13-week cycles.

Why are some people more resilient than others? How do the most successful people and organizations remain at the top of their industry, division, or league? They have a process, support system, and people to help them. And they are empowered most by knowing their purpose and putting it to work.

As Mark Twain once said, *"There are basically two types of people. People who accomplish things, and people who claim to have accomplished things. The first group is less crowded."*

How you show up every day determines the level of trust you create. How steadfast are you as a leader or manager? Steadfastness is a virtue of dutiful resolve. You learn to be unwavering, even during the darkest hour.

Overcoming Fear and Procrastination

Did you know that humans are born with two instinctual fears? The first is the fear of falling. The second is the fear of loud noises. These are biological functions that help us survive. We create all other fears consciously and unconsciously.

Humans create imaginary fear such as public speaking, heights, enclosed spaces, and flying in planes. Why? Fear, like all other emotions, happens because of our beliefs. Our beliefs happen because of our conditioning. Since kids have to depend on parents and others to raise us, we end up sharing the values and beliefs of those who raised us. It is possible to change what we believe given the desire.

It's important to know most of us never choose what we believe. We can condition ourselves and others to think and believe many things. We must choose our environments wisely. Conditioning explains why I grew up to be an entrepreneur by modeling my parents and other role models. Conditioning explains why we believe what we do.

Given the will and commitment, there is always a way to improve our minds and condition ourselves to be more resilient, clear and energized. The key is believing. We can change our minds and reprogram the subconscious mind by learning and practicing relaxation and other techniques you'll find at the end of this book.

Don't take my word for it. Bruce Lipton is a Ph.D., biologist, author, and pioneer in the science of Epigenetics. He's one of the first in science and academics to teach us we are products of our environment. Like Gallwey, Dr. Lipton sheds light on alternative ways to leverage the inner game for success.

What we perceive affects our biological ability to adapt to our environments and seek optimal operating states. Consider the power of the Placebo Effect as another example. What we believe matters.[8] If you believe you're in the right business, and your business is worth investing in, you'll have no problems practicing the strategic action planning process in my book.

Resilience

Champions are resilient because of their purpose. They are driven by their passion and purpose. Their courage comes from within, they work with their teams to get results.

When people work together better, the company is more resilient. Look at each person you employ as one node in your network. Your network is only as good as the combined quality of the nodes. Nodes that align together can help each other become more resilient.

---

[8] https://www.brucelipton.com/what-epigenetics

You need a team of willing, able, and resilient people to help you. The better you recruit, hire, onboard, coach, love, nurture, and fire those who can't or won't keep their commitments, the faster you will improve results.

If you've felt overwhelmed and defeated, maybe it's because you expected to get too much done in too little time. Or maybe self-doubt and fear got the best of you. Sometimes, things that go wrong in business are far beyond our control, such as all acts of God. Learn to control what you can. Let go of the rest.

Fear is by far the deadliest of all mindsets. One lesson I learned while managing my digital marketing agency was that the greater the fear of failure, the faster people would stop working to implement the new actions. That's why marketing, advertising, and promotions are some first cutbacks business owners make when sales slow, and that's the kiss of death.

Be aware of how impatience, an early form of fear, and unrealistic expectations can crush your spirit and those around you. You need to be clear and patient regarding marketing, advertising, sales development, pipeline management, brand building, and all the other essential aspects of growing a successful organization. There's no way to achieve lasting overnight success.

You're still reading this book because you want, need, and expect to learn something useful. Practice overcoming fear with your new, positive mindset and clarity habits, and you'll experience much better results.

Imagine ending most of your fear, self-doubt and negative self-talk. How much would that be worth to you and your people? Every new bit of clarity helps you execute more confidently.

You can make lots of progress, even if you never feel that burning-bush experience of radical clarity. That will be your bonus if it happens like it has for me and many other business owners who have completed this process.

The "Inner Game" Is the Way to Clarity

Your ability to develop your subconscious and conscious thinking will be one of the biggest benefits of finishing this book. Knowing where your best thinking happens will shift you into a higher gear.

If you've ever read the books, *The Inner Game of Tennis* or *The Inner Game of Golf* or *The Inner Game of Stress* by Timothy Gallwey, you know about the flow state and how to get it. If not, flow state is basically about getting your head in the right place for performance—it's energized focus. Or, as the pros say, "You're in the zone." The way to get it is to cultivate clarity by focusing on the process you're learning. You master the art of doing what you do best.

Gallwey was the first author to open my mind to the power of letting go of mechanical thinking and allowing my subconscious mind to run the show. Reading *The Inner Game of Tennis* helped me win major matches and championships competing in college and beyond. I learned how to quiet my critical thinking and negative self-talk by being aware and making better choices.

Healthy Habits Make Better Leaders

Business owners, leaders, managers, and employees can benefit from practicing inner game techniques like conscious breathing, visualization, mindfulness, meditation, yoga, and intense practice sessions or workouts followed by recovery.

You need not be a brain surgeon to rewire your brain, and get a grip on your emotions. Many of the habits you'll learn about at the end of this book reconditioned the human mind and body in profound ways.

The difference between winners and losers is seldom ability. It's how we condition ourselves, our drive, purpose, character, and values. It's who we are. How about you?

Here's a list of benefits you can expect to achieve by working on your inner game as part of your strategic planning focus for business. The better you think, the better your business will run.

1. You will condition yourself to make better conscious and unconscious choices by reading, learning about, and practicing new inner game habits with training, coaching, and conditioning.
2. You will be more resilient, less-edgy and fearful, able to recover from stress faster, and clearer in your thinking.
3. Your awareness and energy will shift to a higher, more positive gear. People will ask you what's different about you.
4. You will be more patient as you learn to manage fear and other negative emotions. Impatience is a form of fear that can crush your confidence and momentum.

5. You will make decisions faster. Results may seem to happen effortlessly.
6. You will exude more confidence and inspire others. You will make it much easier to follow you.
7. Your people will feel and perform better when you do. Everything flows from the top down, and all around.
8. You will simplify everything. Because of this, you will get more done in less time by doing what is essential.

Peak Mindset Potential

One of the greatest benefits of clarity is helping everyone yourself and everyone around you reach their potential. The science of superhuman performance reveals the incredible power of the human mind, both conscious and subconscious.

Leaders are people who achieve goals with and through others. When people align with a plan of action and share core values, results happen. If we take a step back, this is probably unsurprising. We see the benefits of training, coaching, practicing, and teamwork when watching our favorite performers, entertainers, and athletes. We follow their success because it inspires us emotionally. Their success always depends on their mindset, conditioning, team and support system.

Clarity strategic action planning is the way to train yourself into your flow state. You'll be able to practice new habits that help you calm your mind, get clear on priorities, and get more done in less time.

Action Step: *Make a few notes about ways you can be more aware of your conscious and subconscious thinking. What's causing you stress? Make* *notes about habits you will begin working to change. Visualize what it will feel and look like to have a plan of action that gives you more confidence. Believe in the power of process.*

CHAPTER 4: KNOW YOUR CLARITY SCORE

"There can only be one state of mind as you approach any profound test; total concentration, a spirit of togetherness, and strength."

—Pat Riley

Now it's time to assess where you are in terms of strategic alignment. In a few minutes, you'll know your Clarity Score. If you've already taken the *Clarity for Business Assessment*, you already know the gaps you need to close.

Knowing your Clarity Score is important because it's a quick, efficient way to measure the clarity of everyone on your team. Ideally, everyone knows your mission, vision, purpose, goals, and how to do their part. That's the purpose of Clarity assessing where you are, and identifying gaps for training, coaching, and execution.

Answer a short list of 10 questions about your organization, and you'll see where you stand with your "Clarity Score." Every question asks you to answer it on a scale of 1–10. Total each of the 10 numbers for your total Clarity Score. Compare Clarity Scores with your team and see where the gaps are that you need to close.

When your Clarity Score is closest to 100 overall, you have the highest potential to get better results. The purpose of practicing Clarity strategic planning and inner game habits is to improve alignment in your overall Clarity Score for the organization.

The Clarity for Business Assessment

Question	Rating 1–10
1. I am clear about the company's goals and expected results.	
2. I am clear about the company's mission statement and can easily remember it.	
3. I am clear on our company's vision statement and find it inspiring.	
4. I am clear on our company's purpose statement and feel it aligns with me as a person.	
5. I am clear about the company's core values, and I committed to them as a person.	
6. I am clear about our company's strengths, weaknesses, opportunities, and threats (SWOT).	
7. I am clear about our company brand, and how we market, sell, and take the best care of customers.	

8. I am clear about my commitments to the plan as they relate to my department, role and responsibilities.	
9. I am clear about the company's measures of success, or Key Performance Indicators.	
10. I trust the people with whom I work.	
Clarity for Business Score (Up to 100)	

Once you total your Clarity Score, look at the areas you want to improve. Make a list of actions.

The higher your Clarity Score, the better your alignment. When people are aligned well, they are more empowered to work together for better results.

What do you do if you score low in one or more areas? Don't sweat it. Once you're aware of how you can improve alignment, commit to focusing on making improvements.

Expect to get better results, stick with the process, and you will. Remember, training is typically an event. It's fine for teaching new skills to improve performance. If you want people to get the best results, make sure everyone is aligned.

Now that you know more about measuring and improving your Clarity Score, let's take the next action step.

Action Step: *Complete the assessment and make a few notes about your Clarity Score. Contemplate the areas you're doing well. Congratulate yourself. Ask yourself what's working, not working, missing, and next.*

PART TWO - CREATE YOUR PLAN OF ACTION

CHAPTER 5: GOALS, PILLARS, AND ACTION STEPS

"Intention is not something you do, but rather a force that exists in the universe as an invisible field of energy- a power that can carry us. It's the difference between motivation and inspiration."

—Wayne Dyer

This chapter is about the steps you will take to get what you want. You will learn to set one goal at a time, and with intention. You will determine the top three pillars, or drivers, of results including brand, marketing, sales, and customer service. Expect to get what you want, and you're closer to it.

Wayne Dyer is the author of the book, *The Power of Intention*. He has been one of the most significant and positive influences on my life. Intentional leaders know their mission, vision, and purpose. We can see, feel, and be confident. We will achieve the goal or come close to it. We always give our best effort.

Success is a game of clarity, confidence, and action. Setting your goal is a significant first step. However, it doesn't get you very far if you don't start taking action with a firm intention to succeed.

Have you ever won a significant event or championship? If so, did you expect to win or merely hope that not practicing would pay off? Most people will agree that champions do what others will not. We either can't or won't learn, adapt, or take action.

Goals, Pillars, Action Steps, Objectives

The best plans begin with knowing what you want, clearly. If you're not sure that's okay. The key is choosing only one major goal at a time. In carefully choosing your biggest goal, such as driving new revenue numbers and increasing your profitability.

Once you choose your goal for the next quarter, choose your top three pillars for the goal. These will typically remain consistent based on your business model and industry. Next, you prioritize action steps that you believe will make the biggest difference.

Embrace simplicity. Learn what not to do. Choose activities that are essential. That's how you get more done in less time. Embrace the diversity, inclusion, and experience you and your team bring to your decision making.

Here are the three most common pillars we see with clients we coach and advise. Read the list and make notes about the pillars that affect your results the most.

1. **Marketing and Communication.** The first big driver is your meeting agendas and clear communication among team members. Then, your brand, website, digital presence, advertising, promotions, messaging, engagement, conversions, market qualified leads, and demand generation falls in place through the Clarity action planning process.

2. **Sales and Customer Service.** Customer service begins at your point of purchase. Your sales team and processes must produce consistently better results on a dashboard that everyone can see. The Clarity process aligns your marketing with sales and customer service.

3. **Recruiting, Leadership Development, Coaching, and Talent Retention.** Creating a culture of accountability and results begins with recruiting.

Other pillars that may be important to you including manufacturing, supply chain and logistics operations, and finance. The larger, more complex, and capital-intensive your organization is, the more important strategic planning becomes.

Once you choose your big goal, and your top three pillars, it will be time to choose action steps.

One of the biggest mistakes we see coaching our clients through the process is trying to take on too much, too soon, too fast. Another big morale and results killer is leaders and managers who constantly change their mind and the plan. If that's happening to you, you need to focus on doing what is essential and best, next.

The easiest way to choose your action steps is to work through each pillar with your team every week. Go over last week's action steps and make sure everyone is accountable for getting their work done on time and preparing well for weekly operations and team meetings.

An essential question to ask is, "What's the most important action we take now to improve performance in each pillar?" Keep asking, working as a team, learning, and improving.

Strategic Planning Process Recap

1. Choose your #1 goal for the quarter. Break action steps and activities down by the weeks and months.
2. Determine your top three pillars. These are the top three areas to affect new results. Focus!
3. Select the most important action steps for each pillar and prioritize them by urgency and due date.
4. Choose several milestones, also known as objectives, for each action step.
5. Test everything. Measure results. Learn and adapt.

Commit to learning as a team. Coaching skills empower people to help others as much as learning to manage and mentor. Keep the communication lines open. Discuss what's working, not working, missing, and next for each driver. Be willing to have crucial conversations. Build knowledge with useful data for making informed decisions that produce better results in less time.

Accountability Adds Up

How do you get people to be accountable? You get them to commit by letting them know exactly what you expect. People willing to be accountable know the expected results. That's when they can commit.

Commitment fosters trust. You cannot achieve your goals without being accountable yourself and fostering a culture of accountability and trust. You must cultivate your mindset for commitment all the time. Be clear to everyone about what's expected, why, and by when.

Committed, accountable people don't quit. And chances are, you won't have to fire committed people who do their jobs.

Think about the professional athletes, entertainers, or leaders you admire the most. They plan, expect to, and intend to win. They train with coaches, and they commit to doing their best work all the time and improving every day.

Set SMART Goals

When setting your goals, incorporate the following ideas into your goal-creation for clarity and focus. Here's the more traditional way to set goals using your head; SMART Goals:

- **S**pecificity (simple, sensible, significant)
- **M**easurable (meaningful, motivating)
- **A**chievable (agreed, attainable)
- **R**elevant (reasonable, realistic, and resourced, results-based)
- **T**ime-bound (time-based, time-limited, time/cost limited, timely, time-sensitive)

Practicing clarity will help you make better choices. When you choose your goals, pillars, action steps, and objectives wisely, you will get more done in less time.

Action Step: *List your #1 goal for the quarter or year. Either way, you'll break the big goal into 12 months. Write goals with intention and expectation to win. Act "as if." For example, "I/we intend and expect to achieve $1 million in new sales, or more, by the date of your choice." Use the SMART formula when choosing the goal. Align your goal with the pillars, action steps, and objectives for each. Keep it simple.*

CHAPTER 6: WRITE YOUR MISSION STATEMENT

"All our dreams can come true—if we have the courage to pursue them."

—Walt Disney

Great job so far. You've learned the power of strategic planning as a process and how to get started choosing your #1 goal, your three pillars, action steps for each pillar, and milestones for each action step.

In this chapter, you'll learn how to write a concise mission statement. It's crucial to make your mission statement clear. A great mission statement clarifies what you do for whom.

We suggest writing a one to three sentence mission statement that's under 100 words. Don't worry about having the perfect mission statement. Play with the words. You're free to update your plan at any time.

Strive for simplicity and clarity. Here are a few examples of mission statements from familiar brands.

- Tesla - "To accelerate the world's transition to sustainable energy."
- LinkedIn - "Connect the world's professionals to make them more productive and successful."
- Amazon.com - "To be Earth's most customer-centric company, where customers can find and discover anything they might want to buy online, and endeavors to offer its customers the lowest possible prices."

Your Mantra Matters

The Clarity strategic action planning process takes your mission statement beyond the standard approach. That's important because a powerful mission statement makes it easier for employees, investors, partners, vendors, and stakeholders to know how you plan to do good. Most of us agree, we need more leaders in business who seek to do good for their employees and communities. Conscious leaders make a profit and do good by sharing the rewards.

Guy Kawasaki is a conscious leader who shares a distinctive method for crafting your mission statement.

As a successful entrepreneur with Apple and many other Silicon Valley companies and a self-proclaimed evangelist, Guy appears to practice what he teaches.[9]

---

9 https://www.youtube.com/watch?v=Mtjatz9r-Vc

Guy is passionate about making your mission a mantra. The mantra is your, "I am on a mission to empower owners to get better business results with coaching and training." You get to make your mantra meaningful.

Your mantra must be easy to remember. Everyone on your team—your customers, vendors, and all stakeholders—must know what you do, why you do it, and for whom you do it.

If the word *mantra* sounds inappropriate, too spiritual for work, or not aligned with your values, find a word that works for you.

The key to your mission statement is to make it memorable and clear. Much like your purpose statement, your mission statement clarifies what you're doing to make a difference.

You need not be religious to benefit from having and using a mantra. If the word mantra makes you uncomfortable, choose the word affirmation instead.

When your mission statement is simple, and your brand is healthy, your marketing communications, messaging, and sales engagement will become more effective and precise.

"What Do You Do?"

For your mission statement, how can you make it easier to communicate your value and help people understand clearly what you do? Let's look at the importance of a concise mission statement for external use in marketing.

Have you ever met a business owner who wanted to improve their strategy and find ways to get better marketing, sales, and financial results?

Great, because that's what I do. I solve business problems by empowering people with strategic clarity and confidence.

See how that works? You probably could relate to the pain points I described if you own a business. Did I come across with a boring, canned elevator pitch? No, because we need to make our mission statement and messaging clear, inspiring, and memorable.

If you can't state your mission, vision, purpose, and values, you can't take a strong stand with your brand. When that happens, marketing and sales suffer. It's a chain reaction.

Here's another example. Imagine you walk into a networking meeting for the first time. You're invited by a friend who thinks you could be a good fit for the group. You show up intending to make a few new connections, or maybe something else.

When you meet people, you shake hands, smile, and start the networking dance. It goes something like this.

"Hi, my name is Cliff Jones. What's yours?"

"I'm Paul Jaeb."

"Paul, great to meet you. What do you do?"

"I'm a fixer."

"What's a fixer?"

"I'm the guy the Bernie Madoff investors wished they knew before they gave Bernie their money."

"Oh, wow. That's cool."

Here's the point. Paul makes it easy for everyone to understand what he does professionally. As a result, he's now viewed by his peers and clients as "The American Private Investigator." His brand and messaging took a small quantum leap. So did his sales results and cash flow. Now he's onto building another company called Redpoint Advisors with clarity and confidence.

Make It Clear What You

How does your mission make a difference for your customers?

That's what people want to know before they do business with you. Can you solve their problem or meet their needs better than the competition?

Make your mission statement clear about how you make a difference for your customers. Your prospects don't care about you until they know about you, like you, and trust you enough to meet their needs or solve a problem.

What is your mission as a person, and what motivates you? That's important to consider because the mindset about what matters affects how people show up and perform. If you had to choose only one of the following three priorities for yourself, which would it be?

1. Make more money.
2. Make a bigger name.
3. Make a bigger difference.

What you choose from this list says a lot about the priorities you set. Make sure your priorities align well with your people. If you ever worked for a person who took all the credit and glory, but didn't do the work, you know what you don't want to be like.

Be a leader with a mission that's clear, concise, and tells people how you make a difference. It's time to write your mission statement in a way that you can make it your mantra.

Action Step: *Write your mission statement as a concise mantra. Make it clear what you do, and easy for everyone to remember.*

CHAPTER 7: WRITE YOUR VISION STATEMENT

"Vision is the art of seeing what is invisible to others."

—Jonathan Swift

It's impossible for people to follow you if they don't know where you're going. This chapter is about helping you write an inspiring vision statement and making it easier for others to help you.

What Do You See?

Your vision is what you see for yourself and your organization at some point in the future. You need not assign a definitive timeline to your vision statement. We encourage you and our clients to be bold in their vision, and realistic. As with goals, it's important to be realistic.

Being bold is a game of confidence. Think bigger consciously and tap into the power of your subconscious mind to determine your vision. If you don't know what your vision is, that's okay. It's normal for us not to know what we want, or see for the future. We get stuck at many times in life because life can be complicated to navigate, especially when you own a company.

Conditioning yourself to be more bold can help win trust with others. Confidence can be contagious. Visualization practice can help, as well. One suggestion you might consider is a simple affirmation or mantra that goes like this: "I see my vision. I feel and trust we have a brilliant plan of action and we're on the right path. I give fear no counsel. My subconscious mind will show me what the way to get better results."

Make up a phrase that means something to you. Be specific. Use it all day especially if you're under a lot of stress or experiencing self-doubt. Nature can be harsh.

Clarity-empowered leaders don't panic; they practice a process they trust, which keeps them aware and prepared. Practice and being prepared is the best we can do, considering the unpredictable path or wrath of nature.

Be Strong and Humble

The stronger you feel about your plan, the more consistent you can be en route to your destination. Just as a mighty redwood tree knows to bend with the most potent storms' strongest winds for hundreds of years, you will learn to be stronger.

Older leaders tend to be more humble because of experience. Many entrepreneurs, leaders, and owners vastly overestimate our ability to plan and control outcomes. I know I did. I also underestimated risk, and that proved costly.

In my experience, we can control very little outside of our way of being. My point is do your best, be strong, and humble.

Trust your inner game and vision. Whenever you feel a fearful thought creeping into your thinking, observe it, consciously tell it you're aware of it, and be with the feeling, and let it go by breathing through it. Do the same with any negative emotion. All things pass in time. Nothing is permanent. Don't get stuck in the mud. Take the high road and remember your mission; your mantra, vision, and purpose.

Now you know more about using your inner game for forming and achieving your vision. You're making it easier to follow you. Use your conscious and subconscious mind to change your business and change your life.

Now, it's time to write your vision statement. Where do you see and feel yourself being in the future?

Action Step: *Write a short, inspiring vision statement for your organization. Choose your words with confidence. Be bold! Define what you see and make it clear to everyone.*

CHAPTER 8: WRITE YOUR PURPOSE STATEMENT

"I believe that the rendering of useful service is the common duty of mankind and that only in the purifying fire of sacrifice is the dross of selfishness consumed and the greatness of the human soul set free."

—John D. Rockefeller, Jr.

Why are you in business? Yes, you need to make a profit. Even a non-profit organization needs to be run like a real business.

If making a profit in business was easy, the failure rate would be less than 90%.[10] This chapter is about using your purpose for resilience, and attracting people to want to do business with you. It's true your primary purpose is making a profit and being able to pay

---

[10] https://www.sba.gov/sites/default/files/Business-Survival.pdf

people so you can remain in business. Now we'll look at your purpose from a higher level; impact.

A powerful purpose with great messaging drives marketing and business success. People who share your purpose have an aligned interest to work with you, invest with you, buy from you, sell to you, and be part of your cause.

If your marketing message was, "Our purpose is to make a profit," how would your marketing work? It wouldn't work well. Writing a powerful purpose statement will help you build a better brand and improve your marketing messaging. You'll be able to attract, engage, convert, and keep more customers and cash flow.

These are substantial reasons to invest a few minutes to get laser-focused on writing an inspiring purpose statement. Most clients who come to us for help with strategic planning and coaching tell us their sales and marketing are suffering. When we conduct our discovery and share our gap analysis, we often see that what's missing is a lac of purpose, commitment, and often, poor marketing messaging.

Think about the power of the purpose of your business. What more significant impact might you have that you do not see now? For example, I've worked with clients to align their non-profit initiatives with their company expansion. We do this by improving marketing communications that tell the story of the cause, purpose, need, and impact.

Cause Marketing Works

Here's an outstanding example of how your purpose can make a difference internally and externally. One of our clients is the president of a fast-growing wealth management firm based on Hallowell, Maine. Jac Arbour and his team at J.M. Arbour broke through with a major growth spurt by choosing to donate half of their 401(K) and 403(B) retirement plan fees to charities of local communities benefiting children and families in dire need of economic support, food, and education. They originally called it the *Purpose Project*. And they have since changed the name.

Their mission is to empower people to believe they can live a happy, healthy, wealthy life no matter how much money we make or have in a bank. Jac and his team empower their clients with education, and they tie a major cause into their purpose-empowered marketing.

Not only did determining a significant cause make a difference for the people working in the company, it got clients, centers of influence, and prospects to want to do business with them. I've seen cause-based marketing make a tremendous difference when done well.

Give People A Reason to Do Business With You

How can you help your customers want to do more business with you? Give them a reason to believe in you that aligns with their needs and values.

In short, make your purpose about your customers. Make your customers the hero in your marketing, sales, and storytelling. You're almost certain to get better results. You'll know more about this in chapter 11.

Cause marketing, marketing with a cause or ambition, can become the primary storytelling your brand creates and shares. When you make your customer your hero, everyone wins. You are not the hero in your storytelling and marketing. Make your customer the hero. Show them how to get what they want and make it easy.

Make your value clear by knowing your purpose. Make it convenient to do business with you. Look at the most valuable brands in the world like Amazon, Nordstrom, Apple, and Four Seasons Hotel. What makes them special and worth a premium price? Value, status, and convenience is what they sell.

Knowing your purpose can help you fix many common and costly marketing and communication problems. Your purpose statement must inspire others to want to know more and be part of your mission and cause. The shared purpose of everyone you employ and do business with is what keeps you aligned at the highest level; serving others in your authentic way and providing exceptional value.

When you have more meaning in your business and your people feel the same way about their jobs, they feel much better at work, and they get more done in less time.

Nothing can stop you when your highest purpose powers you. If something isn't working well, fear not. As you develop more clarity and confidence, you will see, feel, and trust you are on the right path. You will know how to adjust when getting off course. The more clarity you develop, the more you will feel positive energy and confidence.

You are the leader of yourself. You have a purpose, and your organization has a shared purpose. Do your best to align them for writing your purpose statement.

Examples of Purpose Statements

The most powerful purpose statements tell the world, "Here's what we're doing to make a difference for others." Purpose must inspire you by aligning the head, heart, and soul of the people in your organization.

Here are some examples of purpose statements from true, legendary leaders who changed millions of lives.

- *"To be a teacher. And to be known for inspiring my students to be more than they thought they could be."*
  —Oprah Winfrey
- *"To have fun in [my] journey through life and learn from [my] mistakes."*
  —Sir Richard Branson
- *"My mission in life is not merely to survive, but to thrive; and to do so with some passion, some compassion, some humor, and some style."*
  —Maya Angelou

Remember, your purpose is why you do what you do to be your very best. In getting to your purpose statement, think about the keywords that best describe you and what you stand for in your company, organization, and professional life.

Action Step: *Write your purpose statement from an organizational standpoint. Why are you in business?*

CHAPTER 9: COMMIT TO CORE VALUES

"The way you get meaning into your life is to devote yourself to loving others, devote yourself to your community around you, and devote yourself to creating something that gives you purpose and meaning."

—Mitch Albom

Have you ever trusted someone dearly because they gave you their word, but they failed to keep it? Welcome to humanity. We all know the feeling of betrayal. We know the Golden Rule. Practice it often.

This chapter will help you become aware of your core values and how stating them as commitments, and keeping your commitments, makes all the difference for results.

When we look back on our careers, what percent of leaders or managers truly stood out in your mind as having been exceptional? Not many, if you're like most people. That's because there are far too many of us who cannot keep our word or commitments. We simply can't be trusted when people can't count on us.

Focus on the power of character, values, and living them as your commitments. Nobody is perfect! But when we live by virtue, good things happen. That's been my direct experience.

Moral Virtues at Work

I know. You didn't count on an ethics seminar in the book. But moral virtues at work are a big deal when it comes to leadership and getting better results. Virtues are behaviors based on a high moral stand. We find these values in the Bible and virtually all ancient religious texts and doctrines. Don't worry. I'm not "going religious" on you.

Nobody wants to follow a jerk. The only people who will do for long believe they don't have a choice. Our job as leaders is to work at peak potential when we're working, and take sufficient time away from work to recharge our energy.

Aristotle was the grandfather of modern-day ethics.[11] His body of work became known as Virtue ethics[12]. Think in terms of being of good moral character. Here's a look at Aristotle's short list of virtues. You'll see similarities between the biblical seven virtues[13] that contrast the seven deadly sins.

---

[11] https://en.wikipedia.org/wiki/Aristotle
[12] https://en.wikipedia.org/wiki/Virtue_ethics
[13] https://en.wikipedia.org/wiki/Seven_virtues

Aristotle identifies virtues in two ways that can help us be better leaders and empower people. Moral virtues are how we choose to act. Intellectual virtues are mental skills that we can form into habits.

1. **Courage**. Face your fears.
2. **Temperance**. Face pleasure and pain
3. **Liberality.** Share whatever wealth you have.
4. **Magnificence.** Noble with possessions.
5. **Magnanimity**. Be generous.
6. **Proper ambition.** Not out of control.
7. **Truthfulness.** Tell it like it is.
8. **Wittiness.** My father called it a sense of humor.
9. **Friendliness.** The opposite of social distancing.
10. **Modesty.** This is about being shameless.
11. **Righteous indignation**. Don't be a hot head.

The bottom line is don't be a jerk, especially to people at work, your neighbor, and the commuter who cuts you off. You need not be a saint. Just commit to doing better.

Being A Better Leader

In an article I wrote for *The Business Journals, I shared* a list of 20 virtues for mindful leaders. You'll notice I use the words mindfulness, consciousness, and clarity. The reason I do this is that Clarity leaders are very conscious about the words they use. It's the science of Neurolinguistics[14] - what we say matters.

Choose your thoughts, words, and actions wisely. A mindful, aware, caring leader is a person other people want to follow when

---

[14] https://en.wikipedia.org/wiki/Neurolinguistics

they share similar values. Act as if, and you'll enjoy the benefits on this list.

1. You are self-aware.
2. You are compassionate.
3. You ask caring questions.
4. You listen more patiently.
5. You know your mission, vision, and purpose.
6. You are clear on the goal, powered by intention.
7. You delegate better because you can trust others.
8. You own and learn from your mistakes.
9. You don't place blame or create shame, guilt, or fear.
10. You practice awareness, contemplation, meditation, and mindfulness.
11. You talk positively to yourself and others.
12. You are kind and civil.
13. You communicate what you feel and avoid favoring personality more than principles.
14. You can have crucial conversations.
15. You are coachable.
16. You check your ego at the door.
17. You will engage on the front line with your people, even the enemy.
18. You believe in yourself, your people, the cause.
19. You journal often finding quiet time to reflect on results.
20. You know how to recover and heal your mind and body actively. Stress can be your friend.
21. You live in moderation, harmony, the middle way.
22. You master your subconscious mind's inner game and power and find flow, clarity, and confidence.

The choices we make as business owners and leaders are for the common good of our family, neighborhood, place of work, community, church, temple, synagogue, at the soccer fields, and everywhere in between. We need to find common ground to get a critical job done together.

Action Step: *Write a list of your core values. For each value, write a sentence using the word as a commitment. For example, "We commit to being trustworthy." Ask yourself what's working, not working, missing, and next action steps?*

CHAPTER 10: COMPLETE THE SWOT ANALYSIS

"Awareness of what is, without judgment, is relaxing, and is the best precondition for change."

—W. Timothy Gallwey, Inner Game of Tennis

This chapter addresses situational awareness as a team of people. When you commit to taking your inner game to the next level, imagine the potential for results when everyone focuses on their awareness of your strengths, weaknesses, opportunities, and threats.

You might already be familiar with the SWOT Analysis. If not, this chapter will briefly summarize the practice for improving your situational awareness and preparedness.

Ignore the SWOT Analysis at your own expense. Sure, you're busy. But you're not too busy to do what you value the most. Value improving the awareness of your team with SWOT.

SWOT stands for Strengths, Weaknesses, Opportunities, and Threats. The benefit of proper awareness is preparedness and alignment for best results. If you already have a SWOT Analysis, maybe it's time to update it.

The Cost of Not Being Aware

One of the most painful lessons I learned while building my businesses was how much can go wrong when I least expect it. The lesson learned is the more aware and experienced we can be as leaders and teams, the easier it can be to avoid distractions, inefficiencies, and losses. We need to prepare to deal with anything that happens.

When I was growing my financial planning and investment advisory business, I, nor anyone in our firm, could predict bear markets or black swans. Black swans are events such as the Dot.com stock meltdown of 2000 and 9/11. Our financial plans had to have contingency plans as we worked to improve our awareness of what could go wrong, and how we could position ourselves to help our clients win.

We had to condition our minds with massive, ongoing training and coaching. Building that business and selling it before I was 40 taught me some powerful and painful lessons about being prepared mentally for anything.

Be Accountable for Awareness

Your culture of commitment and accountability demands that everyone commits to greater awareness, learning, and the sharing of timely, relevant, and helpful knowledge. As you're about to see, your branding and go-to-market plan will rely heavily on knowing what you can and can't do together.

The SWOT Analysis is best done as a team. If you haven't decided who to invite into the strategic planning process, consider who can help you most with SWOT, and invite them to help you with your entire plan.

The more experienced and diverse your team, the easier it will be to conduct a thorough analysis. Discuss the best ways to leverage your strengths, overcome weaknesses, create and seize business opportunities, and improve your awareness of threats. Keep an open mind and heart.

The SWOT Analysis

Here are the four questions to discuss with your team. We suggest updating your SWOT Analysis at least quarterly. Being aware is a commitment you make to help your team reach its goals with the least stress and cost.

1. What are your strengths and how do they matter?
2. What are your weaknesses and how do they matter?
3. Where do you see the best opportunities to gain a competitive advantage?
4. What threats do you expect, and how will you prepare to avoid negative consequences?

Now that you know the power of awareness, it's time to complete your SWOT Analysis on our own. Then invite your people to help you be even better prepared for opportunities.

Action Step: *Create a simple list or grid to complete your SWOT Analysis. Thoroughly consider your strengths, weaknesses, opportunities, and threats. Discuss SWOT with your smartest people. Explore what's working, not working, missing, and next.*

CHAPTER 11: BRAND AND GO-TO-MARKET PLAN

"The essence of strategy is choosing what not to do."

—Michael Porter

Think strategically. Act tactically. That's what this chapter is about. You will learn to take essential action steps for optimal results with your brand, marketing, sales, and financial results.

Your brand and go-to-market action plan go together. First, you'll review and refresh your brand if you're already in business. If you're a startup or starting over, use the branding list to to build a new brand.

Don't let chapter overwhelm or intimidate you. You will not figure out all the ways to strengthen your brand, be more mindful with marketing, and transform your sales culture overnight. You're going to read through this chapter and start making a list of additional action steps.

There are three lists of discovery questions to help you plan next action steps for each of your three pillars. Remember, you've got one big goal, three pillars that drive results, and action steps with objectives for each pillar. The top three pillars are typically marketing, sales and customer service, and developing people.

Recap of Goal Setting Process

Let's recap the goal setting process we covered earlier before we cover brand, marketing, and sales in your go-to-market planning.

1. You have one, big goal. It's typically a revenue goal.
2. You have three core pillars such as marketing, sales, customer service, and developing your people. Pillars are the areas for serious action planning and improvement.
3. You are creating a list of additional action steps to prioritize taking with clarity and confidence.
4. You are assigning milestones or objectives for each action step.

The work you do in this chapter is the heaviest lifting you'll do during writing your strategic action plan. You need not be an expert in branding, marketing, sales, or technology if you know how to hire the best people to work for you within your budget.

I will do my best to give you the fundamentals to evaluate your pillars and action steps. It would be easy to write three books to properly cover brand, marketing, and sales.

Your Brand and Go-to-Market Plan Will Integrate

Here are the three checklists you'll see in order.

1. **Brand Builder Checklist** - Use this checklist to create a list of actions to take for your marketing and sales pillars.
2. **Mindful Marketing Checklist** - Use this checklist to create a list of actions specifically for traditional and digital marketing.
3. **Authentic Sales Enablement Checklist** - Use this checklist to create a list of actions to improve sales engagement, sales pipeline conversions, and top-line results.

Brand Building Discovery Questions

The first checklist you'll read through is for brand building. Once you have a strong brand foundation, you'll focus on the mindful marketing and authentic sales checklists. Don't skip over the brand elements. Everything you do to build a stronger brand will help you in marketing, sales, and customer service.

Do you believe it's an accident Apple, Coca Cola, and every Fortune 1000 company invests millions to ensure their brand is consistent and dominant? No, it's not.

As you'll soon see, if you don't build a powerful brand, you'll miss the key ingredients such as your mission, vision, and purpose. You won't have a foundation and you will flounder in sales and marketing, mostly.

The purpose of your brand is to be the foundation for your marketing communications, customer service, sales, finance, and all aspects of your business success.

Go through the list of discovery questions and start making notes and prioritizing next action steps for improving your brand.

1. What are your brand design or refresh goals?
2. What is the market opportunity?
3. What is your mission?
4. What is your vision?
5. What is your purpose?
6. What are your values?
7. What is the essence of your brand?
8. What is the vibe of your brand?
9. What is the voice of your brand?
10. What are reasons to believe in your brand?
11. What is your brand messaging?
12. What is your company's description? (We suggest crafting a 100, 20, and 20 word version of the same description.)
13. What is the brand tagline?
14. What are the brand benefits?
15. What is your Unique Selling Proposition? (Positioning statement)
16. What are your brand personas? (Ideal customers)
17. What does your brand mood board look like in terms of images, examples, ideas?
18. What are your existing brand assets?
19. What will your logo look like?

20. What is your color palette?
21. What is the list of proposed brand changes?
22. What's next for prioritized action steps?
23. Who owns the actions, and what's the deadline?

How to Improve Marketing Results

Mindful marketing means you learn how to simplify marketing and do only what is essential for maintaining your brand reputation, and improving sales, and financial results.

I became a marketing specialist by watching my father market his businesses. He was a brilliant marketer and role model. I learned to look at marketing differently when I was investing my money to build my first business; the financial planning and wealth management business. Before that, I was a corporate sales and marketing executive. I was given a budget and told to plan wisely. The way to learn how to be mindful of marketing is to look at every dollar you put into marketing campaigns and talent as an investment.

When marketing is managed mindfully, it pays for itself. We see the same thing when hiring top producers. We'll keep them forever when we find great producers.

Even though most business owners agree we need to invest in people, marketing, sales, and technology, fear holds us back. At times, it crushes us our confidence for marketing, and in the worst-case scenarios, we give up and tell ourselves "marketing doesn't work."

Believe in marketing and do it with discipline to get results. The same is true for sales. It's all a game of confidence; your inner game. Even the most conservative finance people will see the value of marketing when you know how to manage it mindfully, with the right people, and data.

The Purpose of Brand and Marketing

Let's agree the purpose of your brand and marketing is to drive demand, sales engagement, and revenue. You'll see how easily your brand elements plug into the mindful marketing checklist. The goal is for you to simplify marketing, empower the people who work in marketing, and over time, you will see improvements in the quality of leads and conversions to revenue.

Go through the list of mindful marketing discovery questions. Start taking notes and thinking about priority action steps. Learning to market well is about focusing on the who, what, why, how, and when using a process that works.

Mindful Marketing Discovery Questions

1. How do you measure marketing results?
2. What is your market positioning?
3. What kind of marketing data analysis do you have, or will you conduct?
4. What is the market size?
5. What is your market share?
6. What trends are there, and how will you adapt?
7. What is your USP, or value proposition?
8. Who are your top competitors, and why?

9. What can you learn from them?
10. Who owns the responsibility to stay on top of the competition?
11. What are your competitive advantages?
12. What are your weaknesses?
13. What is your pricing strategy?
14. What is your brand essence?
15. How can you improve content and digital marketing including your website, blog, and online presence?
16. How could marketing automation or AI help you?
17. How could you improve advertising results?
18. How could you improve other promotions?
19. How could you improve email marketing results?
20. How could you improve direct marketing results including direct mail, events, media?
21. How could you improve video marketing production and results?
22. How could you improve social media marketing and results?
23. How could you improve public relations exposure?
24. How could you improve customer service?
25. How could you improve customer appreciation and referral marketing?
26. What other action could we take to get better marketing results?
27. What is missing with marketing coaching and training?
28. What's next for prioritized action steps?

Empowering An Authentic Sales Force

This section of the chapter will help you consider ways to improve sales results. Nobody can transform a sales force and culture and results overnight.

Authentic sales leaders and salespeople do what is right for their customers and coworkers. They are typically cheerful people who invest in learning, training, and coaching because sales is the lifeblood of finding and keeping customers.

Hiring, paying, and firing salespeople is an art I love to practice. For finding and keeping the right salespeople, you need to be careful. For example, when I worked with legendary leader and author Harvey Mackay to build his online academy, the mantra was always, "Hire hungry fighters." Harvey was adamant about hiring three qualities for salespeople, "Hungry fighter. Hungry fighter. Hungry fighter."

Pay Well, Fire Fast

Give your sales compensation plan careful consideration. Your compensation plan has to be good for your business and enable you to recruit, hire, and keep top producers. I've seldom found that commission-only salespeople remain loyal or productive for long. The reason it is best to afford proper base-level compensation is to give your revenue producers sufficient income until they can build a decent pipeline and start bringing in revenue. Every business has a sales cycle. Tailor your hiring and compensation because one size never fits all in sales.

If you hire the right salespeople and empower them, they always pay for themselves. That's why we encourage our clients to pay careful attention to the activities of a new salesperson for the first 90 days. That's when you'll see their best work, or not. Learn to let go of the wrong people sooner. This enables you to hire top producers more consistently.

The best sales teams begin with your recruiting. If you hire sales talent with your head, and put in place a solid compensation plan, you've got a significant chance of improving your sales results and salesperson retention.

Great Sales Producers Make Lousy Leaders

Have you ever hired or promoted a top sales producer to be a leader or manager, and it didn't work out? It's a common and costly mistake when we fall in love with a sales producer without knowing the differences between the role of revenue producers compared to leaders and managers. Leaders and managers take a team approach. Top producers often take a lone wolf approach; they want to be alone.

That's why one of the most important aspects of sales team success is the sales leadership, hiring, and coaching. Hiring and keeping salespeople is an art. In fact, managing salespeople can become so maddening, many small business owners give up and do it all themselves.

Like with all hiring, know the job well to hire effectively. As a lifelong salesperson, sales trainer, recruiter, manager, and coach, I know sales because I love helping people get what they want. If you don't have the desire or ability to lead the sales recruiting and coaching, find someone you trust who has a track record of success.

Authentic Sales Discovery Questions

Read through the following list and make a list of ways to improve your sales force, culture, and performance.

1. How do you measure sales success?
2. How can you improve your recruiting process?
3. How much is sales turnover costing you?
4. How can you reduce turnover?
5. How can you empower salespeople better at onboarding, and beyond with coaching and training?
6. How do you hold salespeople accountable to their activity goals?
7. What resources could empower salespeople to produce better results?
8. What is your sales process?
9. How do you manage leads, prospects, and follow up?
10. How can you better use sales systems such as customer relationship management software?
11. How could you lead better sales meetings?
12. How can you align with marketing better?
13. What could you do to reach new prospects you're not reaching now?
14. How could you generate more referrals?
15. How much do you know about your customers that your competition doesn't?
16. What potential is there for new sales channels, partnerships, etc.?

17. What is missing with sales coaching and training?

Putting It All Together

Imagine, what would it be like to have everyone aligned and empowered with clarity and confidence? Trust the action planning process, hire people you can trust, and tap into the power of your inner game; the subconscious mind.

It's impossible to build your company without the right people working on your team in these areas. Even though I've been a lifelong salesperson and marketer, I constantly hire and pay freelancers to help me do the most specialized work I delegate.

In summary, you are learning to put a phenomenal plan of action together. Don't give up. You can do this. Focus on continual execution of your process. Use the tools that suit the team best. Ditch the rest.

Action Step: *You will need to revisit this chapter more than once. List the action steps for branding, marketing, and sales you and your people believe will make the most significant difference. Plan to win. What's working, not working, missing, and next?*

CHAPTER 12: HIRE WITH YOUR HEAD

"If you pay peanuts, you get monkeys."

—Chinese Proverb

Very few people work for money alone. As a business owner and leader, my biggest and most costly mistakes happened when I hired the wrong people.

In this chapter, we'll cover a few of the biggest lessons I've learned to hire and recruit over the last 30 years. I continue to hire people for my company, recruit new business coaches, and coach clients through recruiting for high-performance results.

My true area of hiring expertise is helping our clients hire, onboard, coach, and empower talented people in sales and marketing. You get better hiring with practice, training, and coaching.

Performance-based Hiring

Hiring with your head and heart is what I suggest works best. When we hire well, we have a better chance of sustaining a culture of commitment and accountability. One of the most-helpful books I've read over the years is, *Hire With Your Head: Using Performance-Based Hiring to Build Great Teams* by Lou Adler.

Lou is a leading authority in recruiting and talent using performance-based techniques for getting better results with hiring. Adler advocates performance-based interviewing and hiring. Both are essential disciplines.

You and your hiring managers must carefully define the roles and responsibilities for all candidates. During the interviewing process, which is to be consistent, everyone knows to ask the questions that reveal the track record of success for the position.

One of the most common mistakes hiring managers make is relying too much on their opinions, making surface judgements, not asking questions that are appropriate, and shooting from the hip on hiring decisions. When you wing it with hiring, you pay the price.

Hiring is not a personality contest. Hire based on performance and for performance. You don't have to like a person to respect them and pay them to perform. Yes, everyone needs to align, and that's what strategic planning is about.

Hiring Freelance Talent Has Never Been Easier

Imagine being able to find the talent you need and never having to worry about being able to afford to pay the best people you can find. One of my secret weapons for building my businesses without raising money has been learning to hire talented, specialized freelancers who help me with marketing, technology, and anything not of the highest and best use of my time. In fact, I am a freelance professional as well.

Start thinking about your best use of time, and how to find, hire, and delegate freelance talent you can hire at a fraction of the cost of full or part-time employees. Naturally, it's essential for you to get advice on how to remain compliant with state and federal employment laws.

Never underestimate the power of hiring part-time freelancers who help you build a better website, drive qualified leads, and integrate your CRM, email marketing, and salespeople into a simpler system for everyone. Now, more than ever, business owners demand specialized talent to get specialized jobs done.

You can hire freelance talent at many levels, including our strategic coaching and advisory services and people to help you tactically with various marketing projects. For example, if you needed a Vice President of Sales and Marketing to help you full time, a Chief Revenue Officer, or experienced business development professional, you might pay more than $295,000 a year. That's $25,583 a month. Most small businesses don't need a full-time person at this level, nor can they afford it.

We established our pricing model to fill a void for small business owners who need better planning, branding, marketing, and sales execution. We make it easy to hire and fire us. We don't have long-term contracts. We charge a flat, monthly fee that's a fraction of the cost to hire full-time talent. The fees we charge save our clients up to 80%. Our fee typically pays for itself like a great salesperson does.

For now, work to better understand the building blocks of your brand and go-to-market plan by going through each list. Invite your team when the time's right for you. You'll know when that is. You and your team will put the pieces together.

Performance-Based Hiring Discovery Questions

Here are some important discovery questions to think about for improving hiring and retention. This list helps you think about what's working, what's not working, what's missing, and what's next for action steps that could make the biggest difference.

1. Where are the gaps now in your team?
2. What positions need to change, and how?
3. How detailed are your job descriptions, roles, and responsibilities?
4. How do you research competitive compensation packages and improve retention?
5. What is your interview process, and how could you improve it?
6. How could better you onboard new candidates?
7. What happens with people who can't or won't do their job?
8. Are you hiring people because you like them, or because they have a track record of doing the job well?

9. How could behavioral, personality, pre-hiring, 360 feedback surveys, and other human resource tools help you?
10. How could conducting reference checks, background checks, help you?
11. How do you know you're in compliance with local, state, and federal hiring regulations and laws?
12. What is your succession plan, and how can you improve it?

These are just a few of the questions you need to think about when hiring and creating a culture of trust, high-performance can-do mindset, and alignment.

Most of us can agree we have blind spots and weaknesses. We must surround ourselves with the people who align with our mission, vision, and action plan.

Now it's time for you to start looking at ways to better hire, fire, and empower people for performance.

Action Step: *Update your organizational chart or create one that serves as a useful visual aid for one of your most-important investments; people. Consider ways to improve your current recruiting, hiring, onboarding, training, and coaching practices. What's working, not working, missing, and next action steps?*

CHAPTER 13: MEASURE WHAT COUNTS

"Not everything that can be counted counts and not everything that counts can be counted."

—Albert Einstein

I'm no Einstein, but as a business owner for over thirty years, I know how to keep score of what counts the most. Most people who invest their hard-earned money to start and grow a business will take their financial results to heart. For me and almost 30 million other small business owners, our businesses are the best investments we ever make.

You've done an outstanding job making it this far in the book. Now, it's time to determine what measures of success are most important to you. Let's look at ways to improve tracking your new success.

The first people I hired for my business were my bookkeeper, Debbie, and my CPA, Linda. Nothing is more essential than having talented people keeping track of your money. Think about your habits and personally for managing your finances. Are you a great steward of resources, or are there ways you could be better by keeping closer score of what counts the most?

Scale and Scope of Measures

The more extensive your team or organization's scope and scale become, the more disciplined you need to be with your strategy, team, communications, marketing, sales, and customer service, and financial management.

In most cases, your Income Statement and Balance Sheet reflect the ultimate score. Your company and personal tax returns are essential records. It's the latter upon which bankers, investors, and partners will test your success as a business owner and leader.

Performance Measure Discovery Questions

Here are the crucial questions to consider for measuring where you are now. You can easily assess your people in a number of ways if you want to get high-quality feedback you can rely upon. It's also up to you to share the financial information you feel is appropriate for your employees.

1. How do you keep score in your money and results?
2. What are the measures of your success and does everyone know them?
3. How could your Chart of Accounts for bookkeeping help you reflect better financial performance?
4. Does everyone know these measures?

5. How could you improve internal controls and manage risk?
6. How much is your business worth?
7. What can you do to increase the value of your company?
8. What's your exit strategy?
9. How do your financial results compare with industry benchmarks?
10. How could you better share your success with the people who helped you the most?
11. What needs to change?
12. What's next?

At the risk of being redundant, the best to improve financial results is to empower your people by including them in your strategic planning process.

You drive performance when you hire, pay, and expect people to perform at a high level. Keeping score is a discipline. Share financial and performance results to the extent you feel it will empower others. It can be very helpful for everyone in your organization to know how the numbers work.

Action Step: *Create a list of the critical measures for your success related to your process. We also know these as Key Performance Indicators, or KPIs. You're looking for incremental progress in the small numbers that lead to the biggest. Ask what's working, not working, missing, and next.*

CHAPTER 14: CULTURE OF ACCOUNTABILITY

"There are no problems we cannot solve together, and very few that we can solve by ourselves."

—Lyndon B. Johnson

As we approach the last chapters, let's look at ways to create a culture of accountability with a dedication to process and expected results.

How accountable are the people on your team? If you want better results, it's up to you as the business owner and leader to create a culture of accountability. When your people feel they own their part of your strategic plan, and they know the results expected of them, it is then that they can commit to accountability.

One of the best books I've read for empowering people is *The Five Dysfunctions of a Team: A Leadership Fable*, by Patrick M. Lencioni. Dysfunction happens when people don't know what's expected of them. If you don't know what's expected of you, how can you commit to being accountable?

When you make sure everyone in your organization knows what you expect, they can commit or not. Then you can hold people accountable, but not before.

How to Reduce Conflict with Tough Love

I've learned tough love being a business owner and father for over 30 years. Tough love is about commitment and accountability.

Tough love means hiring with your head. It also means you must fire with your head if you've done everything you can to empower success. In a culture of accountability, there is less conflict and dysfunction by design. When you align mutual interests, and people share values as commitments, people trust each other.

When trust happens, open communication and honesty happens. People feel safe making mistakes. That's how you can reduce conflict with tough love. Make boundaries, rules of engagement, activities, results, and accountabilities clear.

Commitment and accountability lead to trust. Trust is the cornerstone of a culture of accountability. When people can't trust each other, results suffer. Nobody will feel surprised when losing their job if the manager is doing his or her job. That's because the best leaders and managers communicate consistently and they stay plugged into their people and systems.

When any member of your team is consistently unable or unwilling to do their job, they must be accountable. It's never easy to let someone go. Approach it from a place of caring and professionalism. You'll also want to make sure your human resource professionals guide you to do everything legally.

Do what's right with people, and you'll sleep better at night with a cleaner conscience.

How to Make Meetings More Productive

How you manage meetings deeply affects your culture and performance. Meetings don't suck by themselves. Meetings suck because of the untrained people who run them. That's a lesson I learned from Cameron Herold, a masterful COO I got to know while I was building the Harvey Mackay online academy.

The best way to make your meetings productive is to define the purpose of every meeting and only hold essential meetings. Keep your meetings short and on topic. Always have an agenda or formula for meetings.

Typically, one meeting a week for team operations empowers everyone to focus and get better results. That's it. Never use lack of time as an excuse. You always make time for what matters most to you.

Like with everything else, practice new habits such as leading better meetings by reinforcing the new behavior over 13-week periods of time. The spaced repetition of our coaching programs is one of the biggest new drivers for learning, alignment, and results.

Go through the list and start making the most of your meetings. End the high cost of ineffective meetings and communication by being intentional and committing.

- ❑ Invite only essential people and be considerate of everyone's time.
- ❑ Encourage everyone to prepare for the meeting.
- ❑ Keep meetings short. 45 to 60 minutes is the most you want meetings to run. End early if you can.
- ❑ Use an agenda and stick to it.
- ❑ Don't permit distractions during meetings.
- ❑ Show up on time.
- ❑ Start meetings with a quick check-in and discuss a win.
- ❑ Focus on your biggest goal and number for improvement.
- ❑ Concentrate on your three pillars and the related actions steps.
- ❑ Review the prior week action steps and update them accordingly.
- ❑ Assign additional action steps if they are essential to improving results.
- ❑ Don't be a jerk. Check your ego at the door.

Now you know more about creating a culture of accountability. Tough love and commitment make a massive difference. Clarity makes it easy for you to align everyone and keep them committed to the shared goal and plan — the people you invest in who work at peak performance.

Action Step: *Make a list of ways to improve the culture of accountability, beginning with yourself. Think about anyone on the team who needs help to do their job better and keep their commitment to the* *team. What's working, not working, missing, and next for making the most of your meetings and culture?*

PART THREE: TOOLS AND RESOURCES

CHAPTER 15: WORKING WITH CLARITY

"Never tell people how to do things. Tell them what to do, and they will surprise you with their ingenuity."

—George S. Patton

Congratulations. You're just about done reading *Radical Clarity for Business*. You're on your way to getting better results when you believe in your strategic planning process and people. Nothing can stop you when you have clarity and confidence. If you hit the pinnacle of radical clarity with a major win, celebrate the victory and get back to business.

The more you work with clarity, the easier it will be to get results. If you've followed the steps and begun drafting your new strategic plan, you'll soon know when to invite your people to own their part of the new strategic plan.

Again, what you believe and expect matters. Take charge of your mindset now by learning to master your inner game with the habits you'll see in the next chapter. As Napoleon Hill wrote in his book,

Think and Grow Rich, "Whatever your mind can conceive and believe, it can achieve."

Will you get disappointed, bummed out, and doubt yourself or others? No doubt. Keep the faith and trust your newfound process for strategic planning and alignment for empowering your people.

Here's a quick recap of what you're learning.

1. You understand the power and importance of strategic action planning.
2. You've started a new strategic plan document that will be easy to share and edit with your people.
3. You understand this is an internal business plan for you and your people to share. If you need an external business plan for raising money or getting a loan, you now have all the pieces to use with your financial projections and capital needs.
4. You commit to inviting your people to help you.
5. You understand the importance of diversity and inclusion for best results. Building a company is a team and contact sport.
6. You are more clear now on your #1 goal, pillars, action steps, and objectives. You're striving for new clarity and making better choices.
7. You are more clear on your mission, vision, purpose, values, and SWOT.
8. You are choosing priority action steps aligned with your pillars; marketing, sales/customer service, and developing your people are three of the biggest.
9. Your brand is stronger, marketing more mindful, and sales results are improving.
10. You are learning to tap into the power of your conscious and subconscious minds for optimal flow-state performance,

including the potential to achieve radical clarity and breakthrough results.

Because of your commitment to read this book, you're learning to create more clarity in business and life. Clarity will give you more confidence. More confidence will empower you to be a better leader and team member. The more you focus on creating and sharing clarity, the more empowered everyone will feel.

The way to empower your people for better results is to follow the process in my book, share it with your people, and never stop expecting and working towards new clarity, confidence, and better results.

Give People the Tools They Choose

Tools are crucial to every job and trade. What are the best tools for you and everyone on your team? What do they need that they don't have? How can you be more efficient by getting more done with less?

When livelihoods depend on using the right tools, and everyone on the team is a professional, you will see better performance and results by giving them what they need and want. One benefit is that more work will get done in less time. People feel much less stressed when they have the tools they love to use on their path to mastery.

Did you know that technology is one of the biggest things stressing us out? It's true, and you can find evidence in almost any major publication. Be careful with empowering people with the right tools, training, and coaching.

Have you ever sat through a new leadership development program or software training class and wondered, "Who the heck are these guys and are they kidding?" Nobody wants to learn how to use new tools, especially technology. We're overwhelmed. It could be true that ethics training is easier to endure than some new tech training.

Strive to simplify everything. Most of us experience the pain and frustration of being told to get a job done and not having the right tools. Our studies in stress and workplace transformation show a robust positive performance culture when everyone has the right tools.

When you interview and hire people, ask them what tools they need specifically to do their jobs. Listen, take notes, and look for the similarities when providing the tools you and your team need. Get a consensus. Choose systems and devices wisely.

Empowering people to work with the Clarity strategic planning process, and it will be much easier to empower your people with the tools and resources they need to get the work done.

Action Step: *Create a list of the tools, systems, processes, and anything that helps you and your team reach a goal. Be sure to take a complete inventory of the same for everyone on your team. Look for duplicate systems, redundancies, and gaps that would negatively affect performance. What's working, not working, missing, and next?*

CHAPTER 16: HABITS FOR YOUR INNER GAME

"You do not rise to the level of your goals. You fall to the level of your systems."

—James Clear

Getting clarity for your business and life is an inside job when you think about it. How people show up is about their subconscious beliefs, habits, values, and personality. Nothing is more important than learning the power of your subconscious mind and becoming the master of your inner game.

Peak performance mindset is a process of healthy, daily habits that become a way of life.

The Power of Your Subconscious Mind

If you take only one concept from this book for improving your inner game, remember your subconscious mind is the key. C.G. Jung and some of the brightest, scientific minds in the world reveal that approximately 95% of our thinking is subconscious.[15]

Jung uses the collective unconscious, not subconscious mind, in his work. Here's a quote that reinforces the power of tapping into your inner game; the alignment of your conscious and subconscious mind.

"The unconscious is commonly regarded as a sort of incapsulated fragment of our most personal and intimate life – something like what the Bible calls the "heart" and considers the source of all evil thoughts."

— C.G. Jung, The Archetypes and the Collective Unconscious

Here's a helpful excerpt from a Time Magazine article to support my assertions about the power of the inner game.[16]

"... nearly all of your brain's work is conducted in different lobes and regions at the unconscious level, completely without your knowledge. When the processing is done and there is a decision to make or a physical act to perform, that very small job is served up to the conscious mind, which executes the work and then flatters itself that it was in charge all the time."

What science now tells us is we vastly underestimate the power of the subconscious, unconscious mind. It is the last frontier for improving human performance, happiness, health, and potential.

The best way to reprogram your subconscious mind is to practice being aware of your choices, how and why you make individual

---

[15] https://www.ncbi.nlm.nih.gov/pmc/articles/PMC4217602/
[16] https://time.com/3937351/consciousness-unconsciousness-brain/

decisions, and how you affect people around you. Over time, you'll learn new habits that help you relax and stay energized, clear.

Healthy Habits for Clarity and Results

If you want to see better results in your business and life, work on yourself. Change yourself, not the world.

Inner game transformation happens over time by practicing healthy habits for calming your mind and enjoying regular periods of deep relaxation and sleep. Be patient and kind to yourself. Keep an open mind and heart. Focus on doing what is good, best, and right for all.

Change is a process, not an event. It's much easier to teach these principles while coaching teams during live, recorded sessions.

Here is a list of the most-healthy habits that we encourage our clients to practice. If any of these seem familiar, and you've tried them with little to no success, reconsider what you now know about potential subconscious blocks you can overcome with training and coaching.

1. **Mindfulness is awareness.** Start with awareness of your breathing, thinking, feeling, and how you behave. Become the observer of yourself. Slow down. Look around. You're going to a new level of understanding about how your mind works. Everything you think, say, and do affects the business of life. Practice being more mindful now.

2. **Choose inner peace.** Stop attaching happiness to getting what you want. Be grateful for what you have now, choose inner

peace, and watch what happens. One of the best tools for inner peace is practicing acceptance of all that is.

3. **Embrace the power of process for progress.** Find your joy in your constant progress as you make your way toward your vision. Don't hang your happiness on the outcome alone.

4. **Practice positive self talk.** Catch yourself when a negative thought enters your mind. Develop the habit of talking to yourself in constructive ways. Be kind to yourself and you'll be kinder to others.

5. **Practice presence.** To be present is to be fully engaged at the moment. If you ever held a meeting with someone who was not present, you know what it feels like.

6. **Believe in yourself.** There is biology in your belief. What you believe, desire, and feel matters. Learn about the field of Epigenetics if you're not familiar with it. If you doubt the power of belief, positive thinking, prayer, and affirmation, remember how the Placebo Effect works; it's real.

7. **Think critically.** Critical, conscious thinking is focusing on what is essential and best for the situation. Practice thinking beyond your thinking. Be more cynical. Ask better questions. Sleep on the big questions more. Know that your subconscious mind will always answer the answers to the toughest questions. Tap into it.

8. **Listen actively.** Learning to listen is an art. Anyone can learn to listen better given the desire and practice. Choose your words wisely. Care more about others.

9. **Be virtuous.** Focus on the virtues that align your values with your word, commitment. Think, pray, and practice the Golden Rule. Do a little research on the power of virtuous living. And monitor your mirror.

10. **Choose your environment wisely.** Everything around you is energy. The home you live in, your bed, your workspace, the

food and nutrition you take, and how you exercise and treat your body and mind have influence.

11. **Block time for active recovery and rest.** Schedule time for active relaxation and recovery. Be vigilant about making stress your friend by learning to recover, rest, and sleep well at night.

12. **Chop wood and carry water.** One of my favorite Zen quotes is, "Before enlightenment, chop wood, carry water. After enlightenment, chop wood, carry water."

13. **Practice being while doing.** Being too busy is hazardous to your health and wealth. Practice being while you're doing your work.

14. **Read, Learn, Grow.** Outstanding leaders are readers for a reason; we learn and grow by reading books, watching helpful videos, and being open to constant improvement.

15. **Conscious Breathing.** Do it consciously all day long and cherish the breath of life. Yes, your autonomic nervous system will do the breathing for you, but when you become a more grateful and aware copilot, you will find reward.

16. **Journal.** Writing in a journal is a healthy habit for actively contemplating anything on your mind. Get your thoughts and feelings out on paper or a digital journal if you prefer.

17. **Exercise.** You need not be an outstanding athlete or Olympian to move more. Commit to walking more, or taking stairs. Don't be a wimp with your mindset regarding fitness. You get to work out and your body loves you for it. Get your heart rate up at least several times a week. Stretch, breathe, and take care of your body and mind better.

18. **Feed yourself well.** How can you feed better nutrition, water, oxygen, knowledge, and people into your life? Ask your subconscious mind to show you the way.

19. **Sleep well.** Quality sleep is a cornerstone for great health, like your nutrition, environment, and exercise. Commit to being a better sleeper. Your subconscious mind goes to work while you're asleep. Ask it to help you solve problems and watch your overactive mind get calm. Let go. Let your subconscious mind do the heavy lifting while you sleep.

20. **Care for something bigger than yourself.** Most of us agree it's never fun to live, work, or be around selfish people. Don't be one. Find something to care about that's bigger than yourself.

21. **Don't sweat the small stuff.** Again, be intentional. Use your conscious mind to train your subconscious mind and you'll sweat the small stuff less.

22. **Prayer.** I pray because I believe it works. Like I believe I am healthy and fit, I cultivate the belief that prayer helps me. If it helps you, great. If not, that's up to you.

23. **Meditate.** I left meditation for last because it's the single-biggest habit that changed my inner game, business, and life. It's easy to dismiss the power of meditation because everyone seems to suggest the best way to meditate. The best way to meditate is to believe it can help you commit to practicing and never give up. Do this, and you will find your way, even if it's just a matter of being more mindful and breathing consciously throughout each day.

What works well for you that's not on this list? If you have trouble staying motivated to develop healthier habits, maybe it's time for you to engage a coach for accountability. Trust your gut. Outstanding leaders have no fear or shame when asking for help.

As you think about how any of these habits can help you manage the stress of life and work, never stop learning how to take care of your head, heart, and soul. When you feed yourself with positive information, a can-do mindset, and the right people to work with you, your chances of winning improve dramatically.

Action Step: *Write a list of the top three habits you want to change as they relate to be a better player at work. Write a short descriptive statement about your new habits and the impact on you and your business. Practice seeing, feeling, and trusting that you will replace negative habits with good habits.*

CHAPTER 17: CLARITY FOR YOU

"I am realistic—I expect miracles."

—Wayne Dyer

Congratulations! You've made it to the last chapter in the book. Let's recap the highlights of *Clarity for Business* and increase your takeaway value.

Strategic action planning works when you and your people stick with the process. What you expect is up to you. Expect more clarity, better alignment, more productive people, and better business results, and you'll get them by following the process you've learned.

You understand more about the ways to improve your inner game and empower those around you. As you continue to practice your strategic planning process and execute your plan, you will learn and grow as a team.

What will clarity feel and look like for you? I'm not sure. But if you're like me and hundreds of other business owners and teams, it could be something like this.

1. A clear, confident mindset for success.
2. Improved awareness of the power of process for improving results.
3. A clear mission statement that becomes your mantra.
4. A compelling vision statement that inspires everyone.
5. A purpose statement that reinforces resilience.
6. Clear goals and expected results everyone knows about.
7. A team of willing and able people to do the work.
8. Knowledge of your target market, and how to win more market share.
9. A stronger positioning statement with clear value communicated in your marketing and sales engagement.
10. You base your pricing on the value you provide to customers. Margins improve.
11. You know your competition well.
12. You take a bold stand for your personal or company brand.
13. You are more aware of your strengths, weaknesses, opportunities, and threats. You can adapt to anything.
14. Your brand is stronger, and it's easier to communicate your value in marketing, sales, and customer service.
15. Everyone's in sales, even if they don't know it. Selling is helping people get what they want.
16. Authentic selling is a mindset conditioned to serve and produce revenue.
17. You have specific measures of your success. You can easily track your return on investment of time, talent, treasure, and energy.

18. You have a single dashboard that shows you the numbers. You and everyone know exactly where you stand with results. Everyone is accountable for results because you gave them the clarity and confidence to commit.

19. You get better results and celebrate the success with your people.

CONCLUSION

At the beginning of this book, I promised to show you how to empower people for better results. Now you know how to create a better strategic plan of action that gives you clarity and confidence.

Never stop working on your strategic action planning process and making improvements in yourself, your people, and your organization.

Embrace the journey for creating new clarity. If radical clarity happens, great. If not, you're on your way to making improvements right now.

Lead with clarity and confidence. That's how you get results. And remember what Aristotle said. *"We are what we repeatedly do. Excellence, then, is not an act, but a habit."*

Thank you for reading *Radical Clarity for Business*. May you and your team find your way to better alignment and performance.

If you believe that working with me or one of the Clarity Strategic Advisors' certified strategic planning partners could help you, schedule a time for a complimentary strategy session at www.CliffordJones.com.

Action Step: *Congratulate yourself and everyone who helped you complete the strategic planning process. Take a few minutes to update your notes and review the first draft of your new strategic action plan.*

ABOUT CLARITY STRATEGIC ADVISORS, LLC

Clarity Strategic Advisors, LLC is an Arizona-based strategic business advisory and coaching company. We help business owners and their teams align for better results and revenue.

- **Problem.** Business owners struggle with strategy, hiring, marketing, and sales. They risk losing everything if they cannot execute. They get beat up by stress, and need to know more about their inner game.
- **Consequence.** Stress, lost time, failed marketing campaigns, lack of sales results, low cash flow, loss of market share, failure - 90% of businesses fail in the first ten years.
- **Solution.** Clarity strategic action planning aligns your people for accountability and results - small business and executive coaching for results.
- **Mission** - We help business leaders and teams get strategic clarity that drives better marketing, sales, and business results.
- **Vision** - Millions of business owners and leaders experience clarity, confidence, and better business results.

- **Purpose** - To empower business owners, leaders, and teams to get better results in less time with less stress.
- **Products:** We offer remote and onsite coaching and advisory programs.

ABOUT CLIFFORD JONES

Cliff Jones is the founder and managing partner of Clarity Strategic Advisors, LLC, based in Scottsdale, Arizona. Cliff is a third-generation family and business owner who has lived and worked in Arizona for over thirty years. He dedicates his professional life to writing, teaching, coaching, and empowering business owners, leaders, and teams.

Cliff has co-authored four books with world-famous leaders such as Deepak Chopra and Ken Blanchard, among others. He is also an accomplished ghostwriter for thought leaders.
You can find his work on Amazon, The Business Journals, HuffPost, Medium, and LinkedIn.

After departing the leadership ranks of Ritz Carlton hotels, Cliff started and eventually sold an investment advisory and financial planning business to a major Wall Street firm. He subsequently began a successful sales training, business coaching, and digital marketing agency. Cliff sold the agency assets in 2018, focusing on strategic action planning, business and executive coaching, and advisory services.

Cliff enjoys spending time with his family. He is an avid cyclist, outdoor adventure seeker, reader, and artist in his spare time.

Visit www.CliffordJones.com to schedule a complimentary strategic action planning session now.

www.ingramcontent.com/pod-product-compliance
Lightning Source LLC
Chambersburg PA
CBHW070053100426

42740CB00013B/2833